KINDNESS

is my Super! POWER

Naris Palmer

Mission: To Proclaim Transformation and Truth

Publisher: Transformed Publishing, Cocoa, FL

Website: www.transformedpublishing.com

Email: transformedpublishing@gmail.com

ISBN: 978-1-953241-64-1

Dedication

1909-1992

To the kindest woman I know, who imparted her lifestyle of kindness, generosity, and compassion into generations, my Great-Grandmother Miriam Palmer.

United States of America

Jamaica

My name is Naris. I grew up on the beautiful island of Jamaica with my mom. When I was around six years old, my mom moved away to live in the United States. She went in search of a better life. I was very sad when she said goodbye. I didn't want her to leave me.

I was left in Jamaica to live with my
Great-Grandma Miriam,
her son Gabriel,
and his family for a few years.

Great-Grandma Miriam
didn't mind caring for me.
We were family.
We ate together around the table and
they treated me like their own child.

My Great-Grandma was a firm woman, yet loving, caring, and kind towards me during my early years growing up. I learned a lot of important lessons that molded me into who I am.

She taught me how to be respectful, kind, and to show love to others.

Her superpower of kindness is the best gift she gave me.

Great-Grandma Miriam loved to travel and visit family in the states.

When she returned to Jamaica, she always brought back suitcases filled with lots of clothes and food.

As a child, I observed how my Great-Grandma sat down on the floor in the living room and separated the many items she brought back.

She bagged the food, shoes, and clothes to give to people in our neighborhood who were poor and less fortunate.

**Then she asked my cousin and I to deliver them.
She was well-known and respected in
the community because of how loving, kind,
generous, and tender-hearted she was to people.**

**I will forever admire her and appreciate
the life-lessons I learned from her.**

KINDNESS

When I had clothes that
didn't fit or I didn't wear anymore,
she helped me bag them up to give away.

Showing kindness to others
is not always easy.

It takes a big heart to go beyond
yourself and think of others.

Although, everyone can
practice kindness every day.

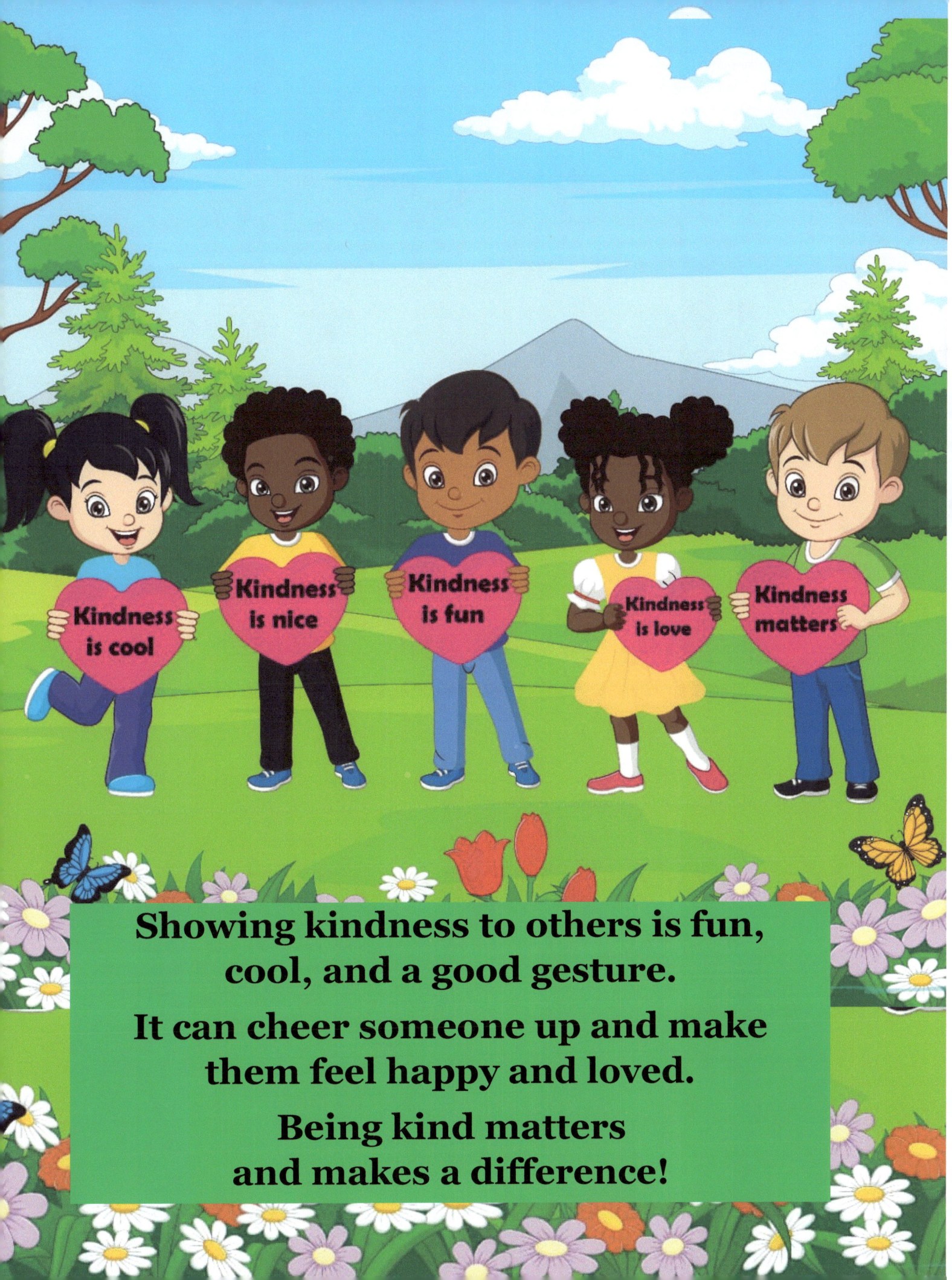

Showing kindness to others is fun, cool, and a good gesture.

It can cheer someone up and make them feel happy and loved.

Being kind matters and makes a difference!

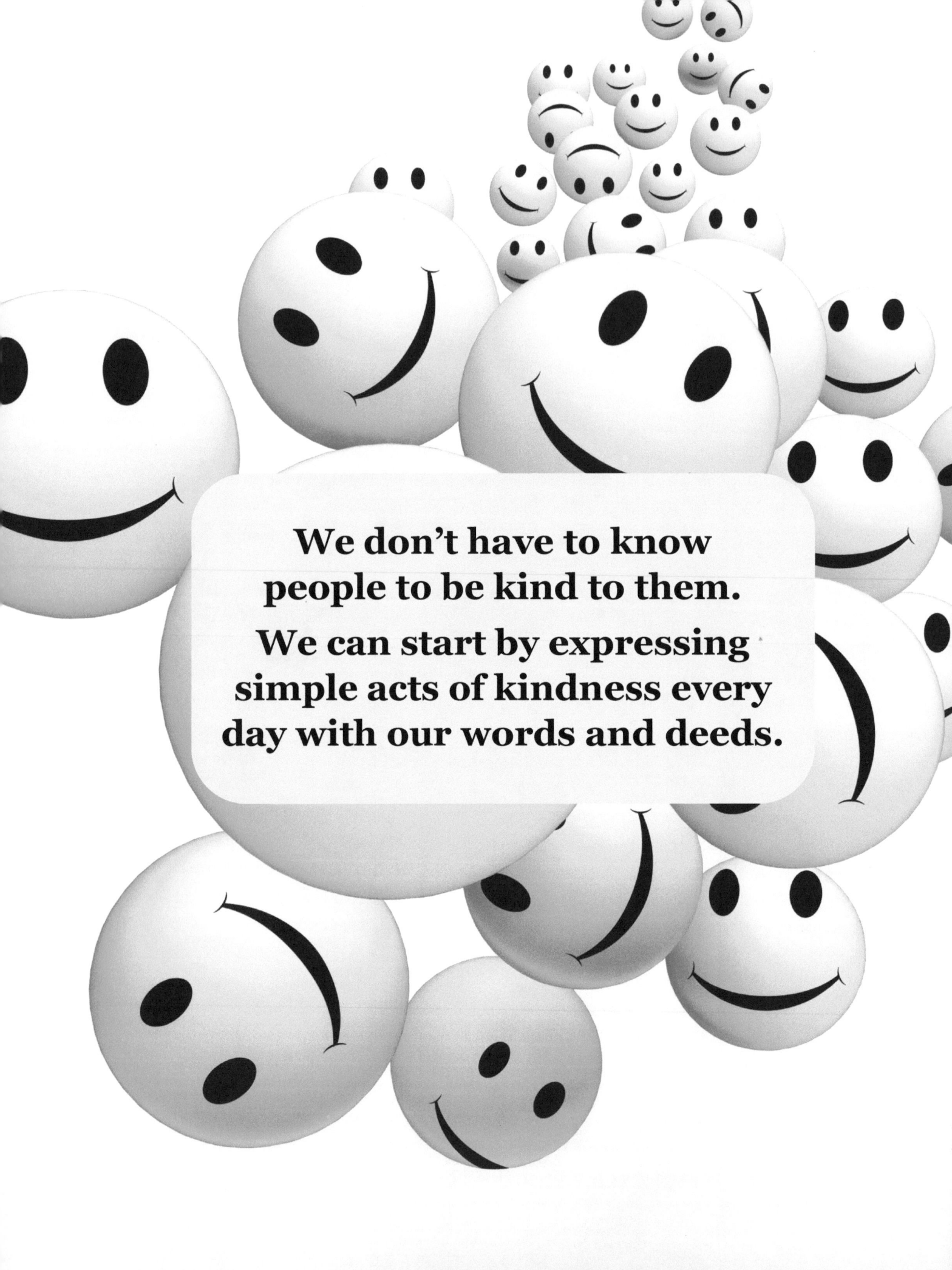

We don't have to know people to be kind to them.

We can start by expressing simple acts of kindness every day with our words and deeds.

Here are some ways
we can express kindness.

Opening a door
for someone
is an act of kindness.

Smiling and saying hello or thank you are acts of kindness.

Helping a friend with their homework is an act of kindness.

Helping your mom and dad clean up around the house is an act of kindness.

Helping your baby brother tie his shoe is an act of kindness.

Putting away toys when you are finished playing is an act of kindness.

Donating to charity to help people is an act of kindness.

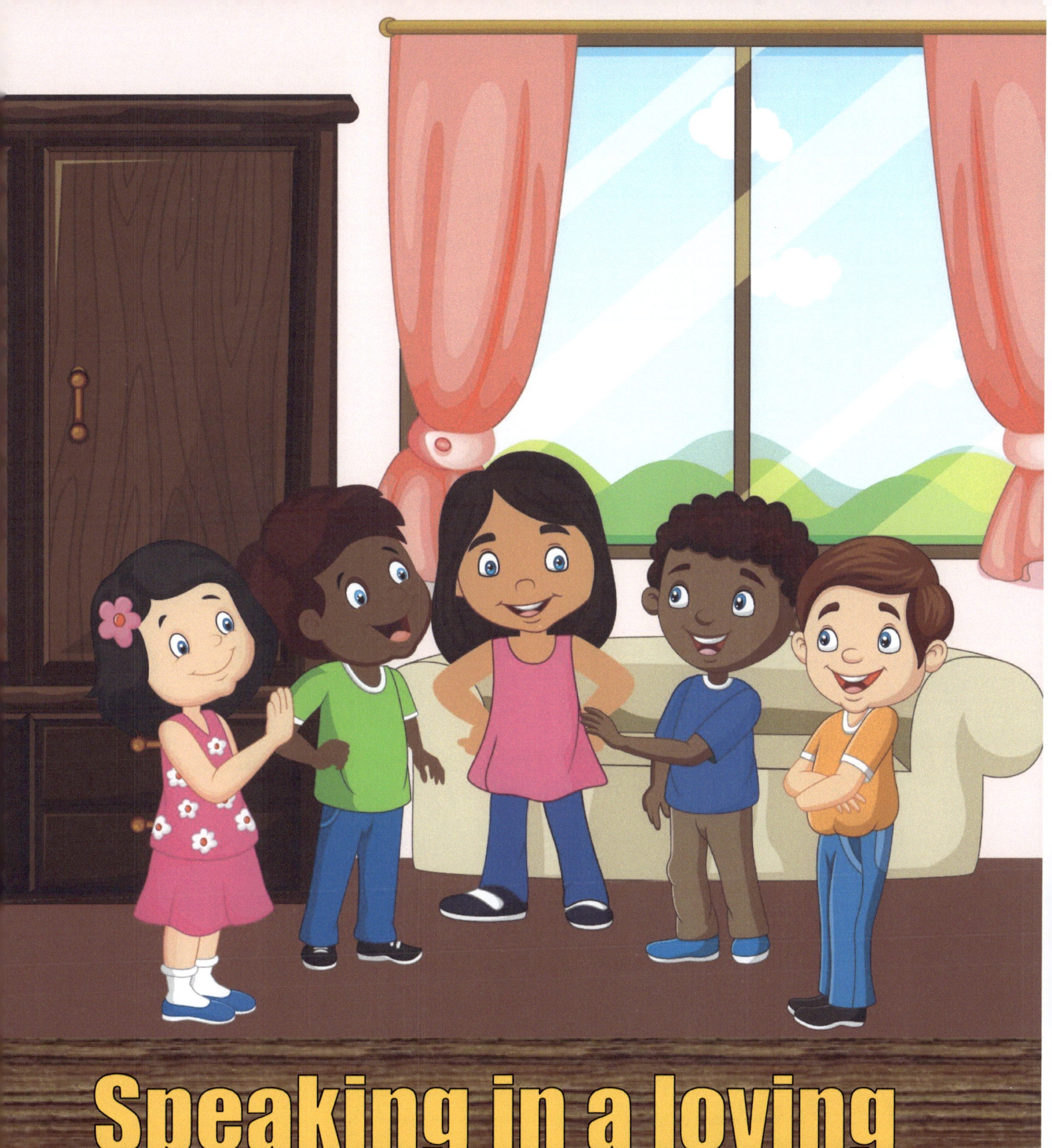

Speaking in a loving and caring tone is an act of kindness.

Showing kindness brightens people's day and makes the world a better place to live and play.

So let's start showing more kindness. Let kindness be your superpower, too!

To my four children Latoya King, Roy Phillip King, Taneisha King, & Krystle King; and my three grandchildren Timarus Daniels, Riyah King, and Ari King –

Always be kind
to yourself
and to others!

About the Author

Naris is an author,
motivational speaker,
holistic wellness coach,
and a children's mentor and coach.

She is a passionate advocate for personal
development and life enrichment.

Please contact Naris directly for speaking
engagements, coaching, workshops,
author readings, and bulk
book orders, via email:

chosenforsuchatimeasthis@gmail.com

LEVEL UP
NEXT GENERATION
MENTORING & COACHING ACADEMY

SCAN TO FIND OUT MORE

Naris Palmer is the CEO and President of Level Up Kids' Training Program.

At Level Up Kids' Training Program, we believe in nurturing the potential within every child and empowering them to reach new heights.

Our mission is to provide a dynamic and engaging learning environment that not only enhances their skills but also fosters personal growth, creativity, and confidence.

We are a passionate team of educators, mentors, and enthusiasts dedicated to inspiring and equipping the next generation.

With a deep understanding of the unique needs and interests of children, we have crafted a program that combines education with fun, creating a learning experience like no other.

Our vision is to see every child equipped with the tools they need to succeed in an ever-evolving world. We envision a generation of young individuals who are not just well-prepared academically but also possess the critical thinking, problem-solving, and adaptability skills required to excel in any endeavor they choose.